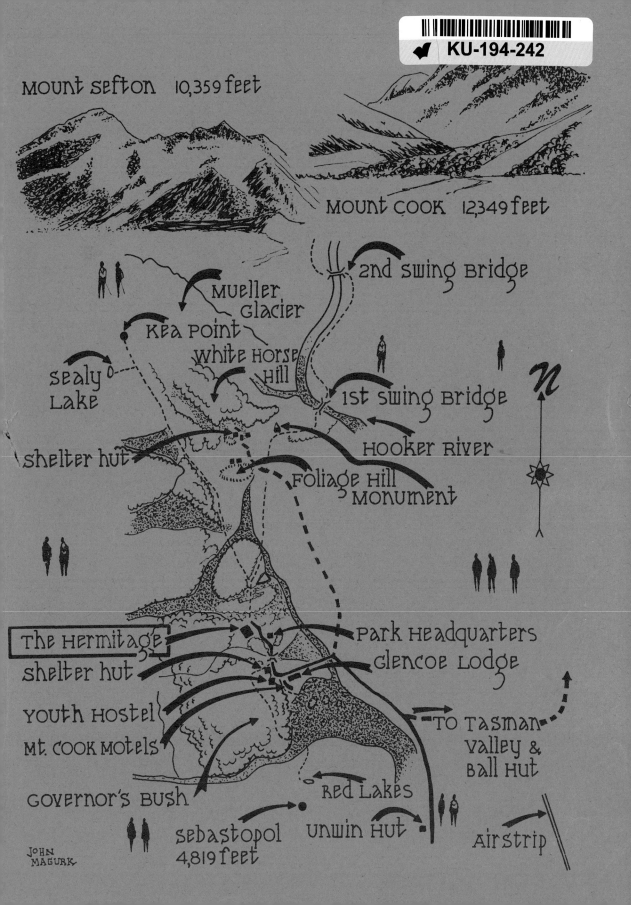

MOUNT COOK
HOLIDAY

Mount Cook

MOUNT COOK
HOLIDAY

John Magurk

A. H. & A. W. REED / WELLINGTON / SYDNEY / LONDON

To Frank Fitzgerald, Frank Cox, and Barrie Maxwell, good companions on these mountain ways; and in gratitude to the Canterbury Mountaineering Club, whose Wyn Irwin Hut has been a welcome base for painting trips in the Hooker Valley.

First published 1972

A.H. & A.W. REED LTD

182 Wakefield Street, Wellington
51 Whiting Street, Artarmon, Sydney
111 Southampton Row, London WC1
also
29 Dacre Street, Auckland
165 Cashel Street, Christchurch

ISBN 0 589 00743 2

Set on IBM Composer by A.H. & A.W. Reed Ltd, Wellington.
Printed and bound by Kyodo Printing Company Ltd, Tokyo, Japan.

FOREWORD

MT COOK is, as John Magurk implies, no ordinary mountain. The magnetism of its many moods calls and draws with all the powers of a super lodestone the climbers, the tourists, the nature lovers, the old and the young—lovers of nature from every corner of the world.

Regally sited, Mt Cook presides over ocean and forest, rock and glacier, river and field.

John Magurk's skilled pictures of pen and brush can at best give only an outline of this alpine parkland which must be seen, felt and absorbed before the full dimensional effect is appreciated.

No visitor can remain immune from this conglomerate of nature and the fact that since the 1870s its fame has continued to spread to the extent that today it is New Zealand's premier resort for overseas visitors. The Mt Cook airport alone has more daily air movements and passenger flows than most provincial airports in this country.

This book, therefore, becomes to the reader an important introduction to that special aura which is Mt Cook.

H.R. Wigley, *Managing Director*
Mt Cook & Southern Lakes Tourist Co. Ltd.

Mount Cook from Foliage Hill

INTRODUCTION

THE PLACE of which I write is that part of the Hooker Valley within pleasant walking distance of the Hermitage and its immediate environs.

The Hooker is no ordinary valley: from all over New Zealand, indeed from all over the world, come folk who have heard of the area and must see it for themselves.

To the north, at the valley's head, is New Zealand's highest peak, Mount Cook. And, even closer to the Hermitage terrace, is the great massif of Mount Sefton.

The old-time Maori knew Mount Cook as Aorangi, the Cloud-Piercer. Today it gives its name to the Mount Cook National Park that spreads about and below it.

The Mount Cook Range branches off the Main Divide of the Southern Alps and is the Hooker Valley's eastern wall, whilst the Main Divide peaks are the valley's western sentinels.

If you've already been to Mount Cook, I hope this book will refresh memories of a happy holiday; if you haven't visited here yet I hope it may prove a magnet that will draw you in this direction.

Meantime, join me in putting on imaginary boots (but stout walking shoes will serve just as well) and come along. As we go, we'll talk of this alpine valley and its history. I've added my sketching gear and you can look over my shoulder . . . .

John Magurk

The Sealy Range beyond Foliage Hill

JOHN MAGURK

THE LANKY AMERICAN comes swiftly down from the big plane. His grin is wide and his eyes are bright. "Say, that's wonderful . . . just wonderful," he says to no one in particular. His flight companions are making for the passenger lounge; he is seeing nothing but the gleaming white mass of Sefton and a sharp-peaked Cook. Already he has fitted a telephoto lens that dwarfs his camera. "Just *wonderful*," he says again.

He is a visitor one warms to. He hasn't put aside the sense of wonder too many leave behind with childhood . . . . He'd have enjoyed the coach trip with us through the Mackenzie Country yesterday: that wide, wide expanse of tussock and the amplitude of sky.

Many come to the Hermitage area by tourist coach or car, but for the visitor on a tight schedule, the plane is the thing. Many types of aircraft use the main airstrip to the right of and close to the main road to the Hermitage. They range from the big Hawker Siddeley prop-jet 748, to the smaller ones that take the visitor on an alpine scenic flight that will prove the unforgettable highlight of his holiday.

Those distant snowfields are no longer visited only by the experienced tramper and mountaineer: ski-equipped aircraft can take you now to glacier and mountain pass.

Harry Wigley, of the Mount Cook and Southern Lakes Tourist Company, pioneered high landings in the Alps. In September 1955 he set down a skiplane—an Auster landplane with retractable skis—on the upper Tasman Glacier. The skis went below the wheels for snow and were lifted higher for dry land. It was Harry Wigley and his men who designed and proved the world's first such undercarriage.

Not far from the main airstrip, on the left side of the road to the Hermitage, about two and a half miles from the hotel, is Unwin Hut, the New Zealand Alpine Club's handsome base hut. From the large windows of its spacious living section the climber looks across the road toward the valley of the Tasman; and is grateful for the pleasurable ease that contrasts with his arduous days on the heights.

Unwin Hut

JOHN
MAGURK

Glencoe Lodge

The first hut was built in 1950 and named after the late Dr W.H. Unwin of Timaru, a chairman of the club's South Canterbury section. The present hut was opened in 1966 during the Alpine Club's 75th anniversary celebrations at the Hermitage, and members came from all over the country to be there: these mountains are magnetic . . . .

Also on the left of the road and nearer to the Hermitage is Glencoe Lodge. Formerly known as the Glencoe Motor Inn, it is, like the Hermitage, operated by the Tourist Hotel Corporation and is serving well in helping to cope with the ever-increasing tourist traffic. It was built in 1967. Beside the main road south of the Hermitage, at the edge of Governor's Bush, the Youth Hostels Association (NZ) put up its Mount Cook Hostel in 1958. Association members from every corner of the world have given thanks for its friendly shelter and enjoyed the company of their fellows. There are also excellent private motels close by.

Mount Cook Motels

Governor's Bush and Youth Hostel

Governor's Bush was once part of a larger spread of silver beech forest. It is named after Governor Sir George Bowen, who camped near here in 1873. He loved this bush and determined that the area should be safeguarded from fire and axe. He believed too that the tourist was to be encouraged, and later wrote to the Royal Geographical Society about the attractiveness of the region. The Governor and his party had as guide one Nicolo Radove, a genial local runholder of whom more anon.

A track through Governor's Bush leaves the main Hermitage road south of the Glencoe Stream and emerges further south at Black Birch Stream. From a high point on the clearly-signposted track there is a good view across to Mount Cook. Above the beech march the hardy scrub species: the mountain pine, snowberry, celery pine, snow totara . . . .

Opposite right: Foliage Hill and Mount Sefton

National Park Headquarters

But now we have an important call to make, a little further up the road and on our right. The National Park headquarters, known also as the Visitor Centre, dates from 1961 and is the Park's administrative centre.

The Mount Cook area became a National Park in 1953 and two years later a Park Board was appointed.

At the Centre you will see displays featuring the bird life and other features of the locality. And the knowledgeable rangers will be glad to give you ready advice about trips in the Park. The Board arranges a summer holiday programme that includes ranger-conducted one-day and half-day walks; and there are evening programmes of slide talks and films.

The National Park Board asks all who contemplate climbs, even minor ones, to play safe and always notify a ranger of intentions: an Intentions Book is kept at the Centre. It is not only the tough mountaineer and the visitor with more than his fair share of surplus energy who are catered for in the Hermitage region. For, early in the Hermitage's history, guides cut tracks that assured the average leisurely walker of spectacular vistas. These tracks have been maintained, extended, and improved; another of the many tasks of the rangers.

So that you may readily identify the plants and shrubs that grow by the tracks, many of them have been labelled. There are more than three hundred species of native plants in the park, and the flowering season is from November to January.

The picnicker, the camper, the day visitor. The Park Board is concerned that all these folk should enjoy their stay: there are shelters with power points, hot plates, and water supply. You'll find one of these on the Glencoe fan, near the Hermitage, and there's another close by the picnic area just below White Horse Hill.

Mount Sebastopol from the Hermitage

In the 1870s visitors to the Mount Cook region travelled on horseback from Tekapo and their food and camping equipment travelled with them, usually on packhorses.

"We understand," said the *Timaru Herald* in 1884, "that in a month or two an accommodation house will be erected at the foot of Mount Mogo [White Horse Hill] by the Mueller glacier, but until then tourists must provide themselves with all the necessary camping appliances and provisions, with the exception of mutton, which can always be obtained from the runholders."

Well, 1884 did see the first Hermitage built. It was sited a couple of miles up the valley from the present building. And how very different from the Hermitage of today it was. Originally built of cob (clay and straw), it accommodated only eleven guests. Later, it was considerably enlarged. Its builder and manager, Frank Huddleston, was a Timaru artist whom the Government appointed ranger for the area. He was a friendly and popular host.

In those faraway days, supplies were brought up from Pukaki and you may still see photographs of the bullock wagons that carried them. Guests came by coach from Fairlie (with a stop overnight at Pukaki), when the first regular service began in December 1886.

The Government took over the Hermitage in 1895 and in the following years greatly increasing numbers of tourists made further improvements and extensions necessary.

An engraved plate marks the first site.

Above: the first Hermitage

Below: the second Hermitage

Today's Hermitage

In 1913 came Mueller River floods that wrecked the old tourist haven and hastened the completion of a new Hermitage at the present site. This second Hermitage opened in 1914. From October 1922 to February 1944 the hotel was leased to the Mount Cook Tourist Company.

This second building was destroyed by fire in 1957. In the next year a third Hermitage rose from the ashes and here (as at its Lodges, Tasman and Sefton; and at Glencoe Lodge, down the road), the Tourist Hotel Corporation continues a long tradition of notable service and hospitality.

The terrace on which the Hermitage is built has taken on the character of an alpine village. We have certainly come a long way from a Hooker Valley that once knew only a cob dwelling and the occasional tent of an alpine enthusiast. Now, beneath the green slopes of the Sealy Range, are rangers' houses, picnic shelter, Youth Hostel, motels, store, Visitor Centre, school, Mount Cook Airlines' travel office, post office . . . .

Mount Sefton or Mount Cook? No doubt there will always be those who will argue about which of the two mountains graces more the northward scene from the Hermitage.

Mount Cook received its present name in 1851, when it was bestowed by Captain J.L. Stokes during his coastal survey. Captain James Cook, the great navigator, had sailed up the South Island's West Coast in 1770 and given the Southern Alps their name.

16

Mueller Glacier moraine and Mount Cook Range from Kea Point

In 1882 W.S. Green, an Irish clergyman and member of the Alpine Club, London, accompanied by two Swiss, Emil Boss and Ulrich Kaufmann, climbed to within a couple of hundred feet of the summit. Later persistent attempts by determined climbers were equally unsuccessful. Then in 1894 it became known that an English climber, E.A. FitzGerald, was coming to New Zealand with a famous Italian guide to attempt the mountain. This was a spur to renewed activity.

Three young New Zealanders, trying a new and difficult route from the Hooker Valley, climbed to the summit on Christmas Day 1894. They were Tom Fyfe, George Graham, and Jack Clarke. Their success was a bitter disappointment to FitzGerald and he did not attempt the peak. His guide, Mattias Zurbriggen, made the second ascent in March 1895. It was the first solo ascent and the ridge he chose bears his name.

Notable early climbs on the mountain included the first traverse of the high peak (1906) by Malcolm Ross, Samuel Turner, Tom Fyfe, and Peter Graham; and the first "grand traverse" of the mountain's three peaks (1913) by a young Australian woman climber, Miss Freda du Faur, with guides Peter Graham and Darby Thomson.

Opposite left: The Hooker River near the second swing bridge

Mt Cook from summit of Governor's Bush Track

Mount Sefton clearing after rain

A remarkable Mount Cook climb was the first winter ascent, remarkable in that Rodolph Wigley was not a skilled climber. But he was a man of great spirit and determination. From 1907 his Mount Cook Tourist Company (now the Mount Cook and Southern Lakes Tourist Company) had pioneered motor transport to the Hermitage. "Wigs", as he was known to a multitude of friends, made the ascent with guides Frank Milne and Norman Murrell in August 1923. Harry Wigley is his son.

Mount Cook from the Upper Hooker Valley

Dr (later Sir) Julius von Haast, alpine explorer and geologist, named Mount Sefton in 1862, after Canterbury Province's Superintendent William Sefton Moorhouse.

With its vast ice precipices rising up 7000 feet (2135 m) to 10,359 feet (3157 m), it is not surprising the Maoris called it Maunga-atua: Mountain of the Gods.

Sefton was first climbed by E.A. FitzGerald and his guide, Zurbriggen, in 1895.

After studying the various routes to the summit, through a telescope from the vicinity of the (first) Hermitage, the two climbers decided the most promising route was that from Tuckett's Col, which is the lowest point on the spreading massif between Sefton and the Footstool. And it is near Sefton's summit, though the ascent from the col goes by way of a steep and difficult ridge. Wrote Fitzgerald: "To gain this saddle we thought that the best route to follow would be straight up as if we were about to ascend the Footstool, and on arriving at the final slope of that mountain to branch off to the left and to follow the névé as far as the great head basin of the Huddleston Glacier."

A rainy night under a bivouac rock at about 5000 feet (1524 m) (when Fitz-Gerald and Zurbriggen were accompanied by three New Zealanders) cancelled out the first effort. Rain and wind and snow conditions led to the abandoning of three further attempts.

Sealy Lake

Down to the second swing bridge

JOHN MAGURK

At 12.45 in the morning of 14 February the two men left the bivouac rock and climbed these steep slopes. Stepcutting was necessary, despite their wearing of crampons. At 6.30 am they had attained Tuckett's Col. A pause for sardines and biscuits and then the really tough part of the climb was ahead. A large rock FitzGerald used for a handhold came away and he fell, turning a complete somersault in the air. The rope, in the strong and capable hands of Zurbriggen, held, though there was only one strand left to take the strain: the rock had cut through two strands. FitzGerald had been carrying both ice-axes when he fell and fortunately he did not let go his grip on them. With difficulty, he climbed up to rejoin his guide.

Though his side was cut and he was shaken, he was resolved to continue the ascent. More climbing problems were overcome and at 10.25 am the determined pair were on the summit and celebrated their achievement by opening a bottle of claret.

In his book published the following year, FitzGerald said of Sefton:

"I have traversed the Swiss Alps from end to end, and I have climbed nearly all the peaks of any importance there, but nothing in their ranges equals the grandeur of Mount Sefton."

"Look at it," wailed the pretty young girl at the Youth Hostel, holding the bright orange ski-jacket up for inspection. She had been a member of an alpine instruction course, and she was also learning about the sharp beak of Mr Comedian Kea. Learning the hard way. She had left the jacket outside a hut and now it was scissored to ribbons. Trampers and climbers have many a tale to tell of stolen gear, stolen food, and even slashed tents, with the bird as impudent culprit.

A popular walk is to aptly-named Kea Point. There the ungainly mountain parrot flaps about the subalpine scrub and the rocks, and gives out his sharp call: *Kea . . . kea . . . .*

So we set out from the Hermitage, where our way begins, and follow the track down to the stony bed of Kitchener Creek. It crosses and, after winding for a short distance through the bush, forks. Here is a good view of Cook, framed between Mounts Sefton and Wakefield.

Today we take the left-hand fork, where the track keeps to the scrub for much of its length till it stops at Kea Point. We cross several shingle fans that run down from the scarped Sealy Range. Foliage Hill on our right is passed, and the way rises (but the climb is gentle and gradual) through thickening subalpine scrub.

A signpost points the direction of a steep track on our left: the route to Sealy Lake. The lake, a small tarn, is in a hollow about halfway up the Sealy Range and on a hot summer day it provides a welcome place to bathe. The Kea Point track continues through a U-shaped valley. Now the great rock and ice ramparts of Mount Sefton take over the scene, and every now and then a sound of thunder tells of another ice avalanche about to crash down the steep walls.

The track ends at a lofty point. We look down and across the Mueller Glacier moraine to the Hooker Valley and Mount Cook. And from here we can see all three peaks of our highest mountain (12,349 feet, or 3764 m).

The second swing bridge; looking back

Mt Sefton from above the first swing bridge

Above: Alpine monument

Opposite right: Mount Cook from the Red Lakes

Another blue day. We're south of the Hermitage and crossing the bridge over Black Birch Stream. Here are the lower slopes of Mount Sebastopol, where the way leads through a profusion of coniferous shrubs. The zigzag track climbs steadily. On a little rise above our destination, the Red Lakes, the track goes by an engraved plane table, mounted on a heavily-weighted 44-gallon drum; and by studying this table we can readily assure ourselves of just what mountain or pass it is that has captured our interest.

In a hollow below Sebastopol's escarpments are the Red Lakes, sparkling mirrors for peak and cloud and sky: here is as fine a pleasance for a lunch rest as any tramper could wish.

The Red Lakes (they're not really lakes, but small mountain tarns) get their name from the pondweed that grows in them.

And the name Sebastopol?

In 1868 Nicolo Radove, "Big Mick", a popular Mackenzie Country character whom we mentioned earlier, took over the lease of Birch Hill station and stocked the run. Part of the station is now included in the National Park. Radove had served with the British Navy during the siege of Sebastopol. Perhaps the mountain took him back in retrospect to the Crimean fortress?

A few years ago a correspondent to the *New Zealand Alpine Journal* pointed out that Nicolo, when in an imaginative mood, claimed to have been the first into besieged Sebastopol and that the soldiers threw him over the ramparts! The correspondent "personally considered the mountain to have been smilingly named after Nicolo's stories"

JOHN
MAGURK

Bridge over Black Birch Stream to Red Lakes and Sebastopol

From the little lakes there is a more energetic climb directly up to a ridge above, for the wider view it encompasses. Northwards, beyond a longer and wider valley floor, the giants, Cook and Sefton, loom large against the sky; and to the east, many-scarred Mount Blackburn (also known as "Rotten Tommy") rises steeply above the flats of the Tasman Valley.

First swing bridge

Our autumn weather holds fine and we decide on a tramp to the two swing bridges and the Upper Hooker, so we follow the Kea Point track till it forks. Today we take the right-hand branch. The track slopes gently to the tawny plain, taking a direct route toward Mount Cook.

We cross the plain and Foliage Hill grows bigger on our left. Feeling energetic? It's only a short distance to the top of Foliage Hill. And worth it, for the view. Out of condition? Well, we'll take the easy track that goes up immediately behind the Canterbury Mountaineering Club's Wyn Irwin Hut. This hut is one of two on the plain below the northern slopes of our hill. They are comfortable huts, as good base huts should be, and the members of the two outdoor organisations that built them have every reason to be proud of them.

The Wyn Irwin Hut was opened in 1956 and named in memory of a much-liked club member, the late Dr Brian Wyn Irwin. Its neighbour, Thar Lodge, is owned by the New Zealand Deerstalkers' Association and it, too, dates from 1956.

Now we're on the summit of Foliage Hill. We're not in a hurry. Among these timeless peaks, hurrying seems more than a little anomalous. We make a sketch that contrasts golden plain with blue mountain.

Retracing our footsteps from the summit we tramp past the camping area, with its stone shelter, to a group of noble larches. Here is Hunters' Haven. Once an Internal Affairs Department deer-shooters' hut, it is now under the control of the Park Board. This is historic ground: we are now at the site of the first Hermitage.

Wyn Irwin hut and Mount Sefton

Thar Lodge.

The track leads up toward a stone pyramid—an alpine monument. The inscription on the square base records the names of Sydney L. King, a member of the Alpine Club, London, from Rickmansworth; and David Thomson (he was generally known as "Darby") and Jock Richmond, Hermitage guides, " . . . who, after ascending Mount Cook were overwhelmed by an avalanche on the Upper Linda Glacier, Sunday, 22 February 1914". The memorial was erected by their comrades and friends. Thomson, a noted climber and a popular figure, had made four previous Cook climbs, including the first "grand traverse" (with Freda du Faur and Peter Graham).

Beyond the monument the track continues across flats that take us to a high vantage point. Here is another view that warrants a rest and a watercolour. The track drops to a boulder-strewn flat and the lower (first) swing bridge. Beyond, the Mueller Glacier's terminal moraine links with the Hooker River. On this fine day Sefton, its mass of ice and snow and rock reaching high into the upper sky, is a dramatic backdrop for a typically alpine foreground of tussock and rock.

Over the bridge the track follows north, keeping to the right bank of the Hooker River. It emerges, of a sudden, high above a sweeping curve of gorge through which a noisy torrent is shouting. The track now goes along steep, rocky bluffs and leads downward towards the upper (second) swing bridge.

Don't be daunted by this now vertiginous way: a handrail offers help to those who doubt their surefootedness, and the bridge itself is but a short span to our destination.

We cross. The far side of the bridge is anchored to an immense rock. Here we turn sharply to the right as the bridge makes a semicircle to skirt the outsize boulder.

The track leads on and ushers us into an enchanted valley.

And filling the valley's head is the mighty Cloud Piercer—Mount Cook.

Whether your preference is for Hermitage or huts, Glencoe Lodge or Mount Cook Motels, Youth Hostel or nylon tent, you'll like the Hooker Valley.

You may tramp the valley floor, climb high or low, or you may be content just to sit basking in the sun. Either way, you'll come back refreshed from your Mount Cook holiday: refreshed in mind and spirit.

Remember the 121st Psalm?
I will lift up mine eyes unto the hills,
from whence cometh my help.

Note

The (outward) times suggested by the Mount Cook National Park Board for the walks discussed, and allowing for pauses and rests, are, from the Hermitage:

To Governor's Bush (to highest point on track) ¾ hour; round trip 1¼ hours.

To Kea Point, 1½ hours; to Sealy Lake, 2½ hours.

To Red Lakes, 2 hours; to ridge above, further ¾ hour.

To Lower Swing Bridge, 1 hour; to Upper Swing Bridge, 1½ hours.

Whether your preference is for Hermitage or huts, Glencoe Lodge or Mount Cook Motels, Youth Hostel or nylon tent, you'll like the Hooker Valley.

You may tramp the valley floor, climb high or low, or you may be content just to sit basking in the sun. Either way, you'll come back refreshed from your Mount Cook holiday: refreshed in mind and spirit.

Remember the 121st Psalm?
I will lift up mine eyes unto the hills,
from whence cometh my help.

Note

The (outward) times suggested by the Mount Cook National Park Board for the walks discussed, and allowing for pauses and rests, are, from the Hermitage:

To Governor's Bush (to highest point on track) ¾ hour;
round trip 1¼ hours.

To Kea Point, 1½ hours; to Sealy Lake, 2½ hours.

To Red Lakes, 2 hours; to ridge above, further ¾ hour.

To Lower Swing Bridge, 1 hour; to Upper Swing Bridge, 1½ hours.

Thar Lodge.

JOHN
MAGURK

The track leads up toward a stone pyramid—an alpine monument. The inscription on the square base records the names of Sydney L. King, a member of the Alpine Club, London, from Rickmansworth; and David Thomson (he was generally known as "Darby") and Jock Richmond, Hermitage guides, " . . . who, after ascending Mount Cook were overwhelmed by an avalanche on the Upper Linda Glacier, Sunday, 22 February 1914". The memorial was erected by their comrades and friends. Thomson, a noted climber and a popular figure, had made four previous Cook climbs, including the first "grand traverse" (with Freda du Faur and Peter Graham).

Beyond the monument the track continues across flats that take us to a high vantage point. Here is another view that warrants a rest and a watercolour. The track drops to a boulder-strewn flat and the lower (first) swing bridge. Beyond, the Mueller Glacier's terminal moraine links with the Hooker River. On this fine day Sefton, its mass of ice and snow and rock reaching high into the upper sky, is a dramatic backdrop for a typically alpine foreground of tussock and rock.

Over the bridge the track follows north, keeping to the right bank of the Hooker River. It emerges, of a sudden, high above a sweeping curve of gorge through which a noisy torrent is shouting. The track now goes along steep, rocky bluffs and leads downward towards the upper (second) swing bridge.

Don't be daunted by this now vertiginous way: a handrail offers help to those who doubt their surefootedness, and the bridge itself is but a short span to our destination.

We cross. The far side of the bridge is anchored to an immense rock. Here we turn sharply to the right as the bridge makes a semicircle to skirt the outsize boulder.

The track leads on and ushers us into an enchanted valley.

And filling the valley's head is the mighty Cloud Piercer—Mount Cook.

31